Business Analyst

Quick Start Guide

A Roadmap for Career Growth in the Information Technology Field of Business Analysis (Related to Software Requirements and Process Improvements)

Business Analyst

Quick Start Guide

What's BA Books All About?

BAbooks.net   is an initiative launched to simplify the process of acquiring valuable, marketable skills—particularly in the field of business analysis **(http://babooks.net).**

There are many resources out there to educate oneself on valuable skills, but **BA Books** strives to deliver products that are:

- ***Easy to understand—in simple, plain English***
- ***Short, and to the point***
- ***Engineered for rapid personal growth and marketability***

CHAPTER 1

Book Overview, Related Books & Author Qualifications

The purpose of this text is to quickly share valuable skills, techniques, and tools related to the **Business Analyst (BA)** role—a field that seems to be ever growing in demand. The book is designed not only for those who are considering a career as a Business Analyst, but also for those who are already experienced. Organizations can also benefit from this short start-up manual, by providing a training platform for employees moving into the **BA** role—a role that is sometimes filled through internal promotions due to difficulties in finding talent within the market.

This volume provides a realistic, practical example of **Business Requirements Documentation** through tools, such as flow diagrams, use-cases, and screenshots, which are commonly used in the **BA** world, and also shares this information in a way that offers insights that help *both*, existing **BA's** as well as those that are new to the landscape.

The book does not delve too deeply into any of the various **Business Analyst** tools used. Instead, an effort is made within the text to give the reader just enough information to be able to quickly grasp the essence of each tool used, thereby allowing an extremely fast-paced, yet easy-to-digest learning experience. The experienced **BA** will find new techniques on how to think about business problems, as well as other insights with respect to dealing with stakeholders and building confidence in one's profession.

The text takes the reader through a realistic application enhancement at a fictitious title company. The example is small enough to digest quickly, but detailed enough to understand the importance of a thorough design. Although typical real-life enhancements might have much more complex flows, the book presents a clear demonstration of critical thinking skills, writing skills, and core **BA** principals essential for the **Business Analyst** role.

A good **Business Analyst** is one who can drill down, ask many questions, and get an extremely clear understanding of the desired goal. In this book, and subsequent **BA** books (offered through **BA Books**), the reader will find a good platform to be able to cultivate such skills. The suite of **BA** books under development at **www.BABooks.net** will serve as an excellent starting point for a deeper engagement into the **BA** role.

The book is written in a casual, first-person tense, as I hope to be your personal guide through this exciting and rewarding journey.

As you read the document, you might make a mental note of how I do not use terminology before it is clearly defined, and this should facilitate very light and easy reading.

The book takes you through enhancements of a fictitious web-based application called **HSH (Home Sweet Home)**. The text does go into slight detail about technicalities regarding web-capabilities, and establishes that a certain amount of technical knowledge is clearly an advantage for a **Business Analyst** to have.

There is a school of thought that proposes that **Business Analysts** should be purely functional. In the real world, however, such ideals are not held to heart completely. Knowing the limitations of technologies can help in determining proper flow.

For example, web applications must have local client-based components to scan data; scanning directly into a web application is not a task that is feasible. Without such knowledge, the **BA** might document an improper flow, and propose a solution that is not possible to implement. These details will be shared later in the book.

I've also touched upon test cases in this book, as it is often the responsibility of **Business Analysts** to assist in writing test cases.

If you get stuck while reading the text, and something could be made clearer, please contact the author at **BA Books** (http://BABooks.net); the author's contact email will be at the top of the web page. Please put "BA Feedback" in the subject line. I will personally answer your questions, and I can use your comments to improve the book.

Other Related Low-priced Books & Author Qualifications

Kamlesh Mistry graduated in the field of Computer Science from University of Houston in 1993, and has worked within the I.T. field for major companies, such as AT&T, Halliburton, Shell, United Airlines, Corporate Express, and Invesco.

Kamlesh's passion for knowledge-sharing encompasses both technical and non-technical dimensions.

He has written a total of 6 books. **BA Quick Start Guide** is his first technical, **BA** book. **Business Analyst Technical Edge Quick Start Guide** is his most recent title.

While **Business Analyst Quick Start Guide** focuses on critical thinking skills and **BA** tools, the **Business Analyst Technical Edge Quick Start Guide** focuses on cultivating analytical skills *that will help both, the novice* **BA**, *and the advanced* **BA**, increase technical skills, marketability, and pay through the cultivation of technical skills related to business objects, database setup, and **SQL** queries.

Business Analyst Role Made Easy, another **BA** title, focuses on customer communication, requirements elicitation, as well as critical thinking skills.

These works are marketed through **BABooks.net**—an endeavor launched to simplify the process of acquiring valuable, marketable skills in the domain of business analysis.

Titles from **BABooks.net** are very helpful to anyone seeking to advance their **BA** career, and are geared towards helping the reader quickly start focusing and thinking in an analytical way. Although the books complement each other, they can be read in any order.

Kamlesh is also a contributor to **IQBooks.pub**. While **BABooks.net** focuses on quickly growing valuable, marketable skills in the **BA** domain, the objective of **IQBooks.pub** is also to grow valuable skills—but with a twist. **IQBooks.pub** strives to impart skills that will not only be valuable for readers on the job, but also in relationships at work, and in life.

IQBooks.pub is about nurturing intelligence and harmony—key skills that will help one's marketability and job growth.

You can read more about **IQ Books** in the next few pages, or skip to Chapter 2 to start your journey into the **BA Quick Start Guide**.

What's IQ Books All About?

IQ Books is a separate endeavor from ***BA Books***, but shares a similar goal—to impart valuable skills **(http://www.iqbooks.pub)**.

In a nutshell, ***IQ Books*** is about nurturing intelligence through entertainment—for all ages.

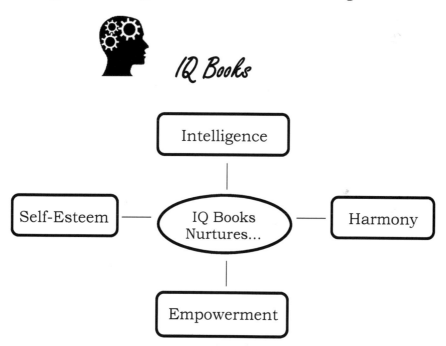

Through the development of products enjoyed by students, families, parents, and educators, ***IQ Books*** is committed to nurturing skills that allow people to better handle difficult situations and get along with each other.

IQ Books strives to create entertaining stories for all ages in simple English that everyone can understand. The stories are meant for both, youth and adults.

There is a growing need for strengthening leadership skills, to create a world where harmony, technology, and prosperity can co-exist and benefit everyone.

IQ Books nurtures leadership skills, by using fiction to promote a high degree of intelligence and self-esteem—qualities that are important for success in the modern world.

By using the mediums of adventure, mystery, and humor, *IQ Books* nurtures intelligence through entertainment.

IQ Books partners with psychologists to review stories before publication, as well as exceptional artists to bring stories to life.

IQ Books

WWW.IQBOOKS.PUB

CHAPTER 2

Introduction to Gathering High Level Specifications

In this section, I will introduce the process of gathering **High-Level Specifications**.

The first step in a process improvement effort is to understand, at a high level, the current process, and the conceived, improved process. This process evaluation may or may not be related to computer systems.

For example, today, at certain doctors' offices, patients that are sick with cold-flu-like symptoms have a dedicated, separate waiting area. This is an example of a process improvement effort that has occurred in the real world, and it is totally unrelated to computer application systems!

Often, though, in the **BA** world, the analyst will be dealing with improvements and enhancements involving computer application systems.

It is very important to have clear definitions and explanations in your specifications.

In the real world, objects tie to each other, and have relationships to each other. It is important to keep these relationships in mind when writing specifications.

For example, when you buy merchandise from **Amazon.com** (an internet store), you might buy 3 different items on the same order: a lamp, a pencil pack, and a bottle of Nature-Made multi-vitamins.

Thus, one order might have 3 different line items. The line items are tied to the order. The order is a "container" for the line items. Let's assume that the purchaser is "John Smith."

The **Purchaser** (i.e. **Buyer**) is tied to the **Order**, not to the **Line Items**. Why?

Answer: All items on any **Order** have the same **Buyer** (i.e. **Purchaser**), therefore, the **Buyer** should be linked to the **Order** and not to the **Line Items**.

If you tie the **Buyer** to the **Line Items**, you have to replicate "John Smith" 3 times, as demonstrated by the next figure.

Improper Relationship Illustration (Buyer is tied to each & every Line Item):

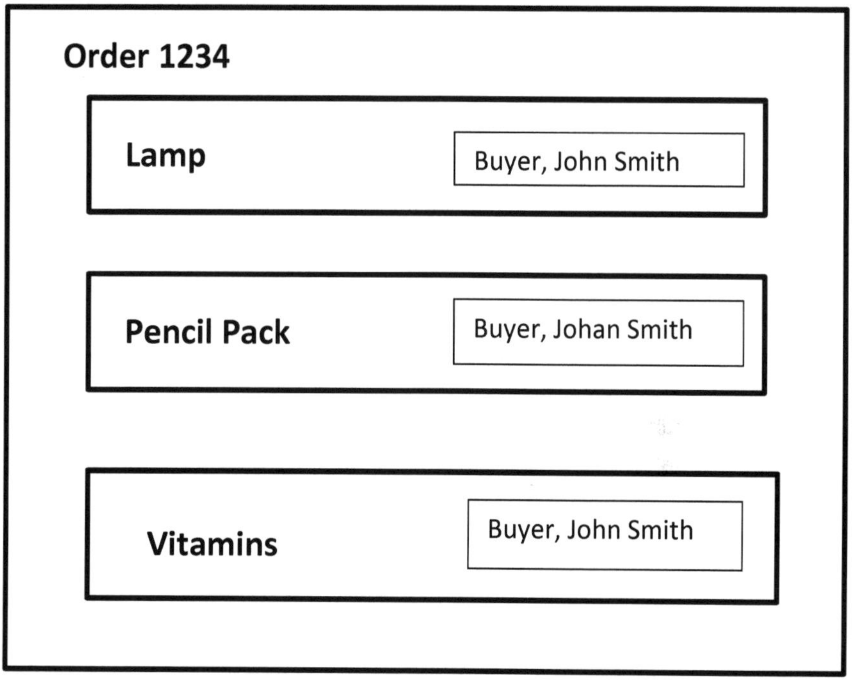

Order 1234

Lamp — Buyer, John Smith

Pencil Pack — Buyer, Johan Smith

Vitamins — Buyer, John Smith

Figure 1.

Proper Relationship Illustration (Buyer is tied to Order & Order is container for the Buyer):

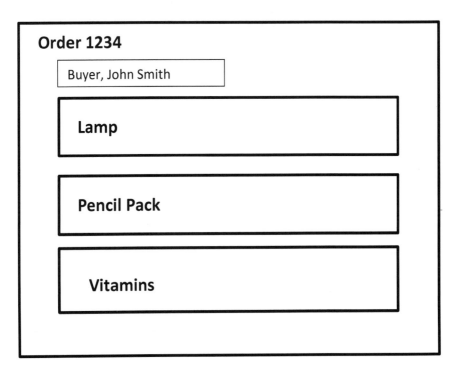

Figure 2.

The **Buyer** belongs to the **Order**, and every **Line Item** also belongs to the **Order**. When you purchase merchandise at **Amazon.com**, you are the **Buyer**, and your information, such as name, address, etc. is linked to the **Order**, and not to each and every **Line Item** that you purchase. If the information was linked to **Line Items**, it would have to be repeated for each **Line Item**. And since the **Buyer** information must be exactly the same for each and every single **Line Item** on the **Order**, it makes more sense to link the **Buyer** to the **Order**, and not to the **Line Items**.

Order, **Buyer**, and **Line Item** are **Business Objects—** data entities that are a part of a business process. When designing **High Level Specifications**, **Business Objects** related to the process improvement efforts will be referenced within the context of **Process Flow Diagrams**. **Process Flow Diagramming** is a very powerful and valuable tool in defining specifications.

In this text, I've strived to not use complicated words before introducing the terminology needed to understand them, however, if things are not clear at this point, don't worry and keep reading. Everything will make sense very quickly, because the examples that I have provided are very simple. After finishing an initial, quick reading, it might be beneficial to go through a second pass of reading the text.

Process Flows are diagrams that describe a process. The process could be an "AS-IS" process or a "TO-BE" process. An **AS-IS Process Diagram** is a diagram that describes a process, as it exists in practice currently, whereas a **TO-BE Process Diagram** is a diagram that describes either a completely new process OR an improved process that replaces an old, **AS-IS** process. If you take a peek forward into the next few pages, you will see examples of **Process Flow Diagrams**. Diagrams such as these are typically designed in an application called **Microsoft Visio**.

Gathering **High Level Requirements** is a communicative process whereby the **BA** *develops* clear definitions of objects related to the current business flow, an understanding of the relationships between those objects, **Process Flows** of the current processes, as well as **Process Flows** of the conceived, improved processes.

Process Flows often reference specific **Actors** of the system. In the **BA** world, an **Actor** is a classification of persons that either engage in specific processes or interact with the computer application system in a certain way. For the sake of simplicity, we will use this definition, although if you launch research into the subject matter, you will find that an **Actor** need not be restricted to persons.

Let's take the example of an **Order Entry System**. One might have different **Actors**, such as **Order-taker**, **Shipper**, and **Administrator**. Each category of users interacts with the system differently. For example, a **Shipper** is not allowed to enter orders, but the **Shipper** can view the order queue to fulfill orders. Only an **Administrator** can go into the **Admin Console** and add a new user. Etc.

The **Process Flows** that you will develop in your **High Level Specification** will have reference to the various **Actors**.

Process Flow Diagrams primarily consists of two elements: **Process & Decision**. The **Process** element encompasses a sequence of actions / events, and the **Decision** element branches the logic into multiple points based on criteria:

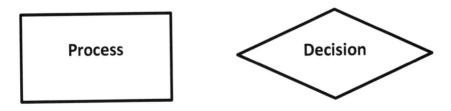

I will give a very brief example of a **Process Flow Diagram** that I believe you should understand very easily. Let's take the example of checking into a doctor's office. The patient checks in with insurance data, and is put in queue for the doctor visit. If the patient is more than 10 minutes early, then the patient is asked to come back to the reception at a later time.

Note: In the diagram on the next page, "Patient more than 10 minutes early" is shortened to "Patient > 10 mins. Early."

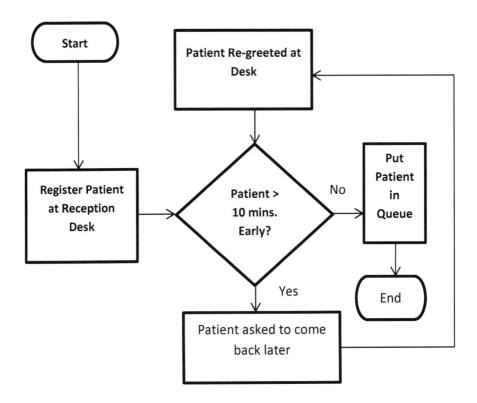

Figure 3.

The above diagram describes the flow I had just mentioned. The flow starts at the "Start" node, and ends at the "End" node. Each process (rectangle) may be a sequence of events / actions, however, the sequence is not fully described in the process box. For example, the "Register Patient" process might involve taking updated insurance data, accepting co-pay, etc. The "Patient is Asked to Come Back Later" process includes a) Patient being asked to come back later, as well as b) the Patient actually walking back to the desk. To understand the diagram, simply follow the flow arrows.

Following the arrow from the **Start** oval, the first point in the process is to register the patient; as mentioned, this could entail a number of things, and not everything will be listed in the process box. The patient's co-pay & insurance card are taken at this point.

If you follow the arrows, you will find that the next step is to determine whether or not the patient is more than 10 minutes early. If not, he is put in the queue right away, else he is asked to wait until the proper time.

The process illustrated is simply a process that an office might follow. As one polishes one's analytical skills, one can learn to spot process-improvement initiatives, which is also a key component of the **BA** role. Note the flow shown, and see if you can identify any process improvement initiatives. You might also identify any mistakes and oversights in the process defined.

One area of improvement that I noticed in the flow is that the process does not take into account a patient showing up late!

Another problem with the flow is that the person who shows up on time can possibly be placed behind a person who shows up five minutes early.

For our purposes, the diagram is limited to the patient entering the queue to see the doctor, however, the diagram could potentially be much more complex— from registration to completion of doctor visit.

For the sake of clarity, let's examine the different objects related to the process. Although this particular example is very simple, an object-break-down is often helpful for the **BA** to understand how objects tie to each other.

We have 2 main Actors, the **Patient** and the **Reception Desk Worker**. We also have **Appointments**. **Appointments** belong to patients, and any patient might have more than 1 appointment on the calendar.

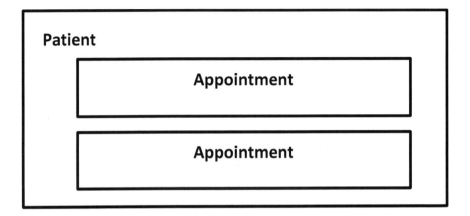

Figure 4.

The boxes show that **Appointments** are tied to a **Patient**, and that it is possible for a patient to have more than one appointment. Such boxes are normally not found in specifications, however, the objective is to develop clarity, and the purpose is mostly for the **BA** to get a better understanding.

Although the figure shows that the **Patient** has two **Appointments**, it is possible for the **Patient** to have more than two or less than two **Appointments**.

It is possible to have other boxes that are unrelated on the diagram shown on the previous page, and boxes *need not* go inside each other. For example, you might have **User** as its own box (**User** is a person who logs into the system to enter / adjust data). The below box diagram shows that **Users** are not tied to patient data in any way:

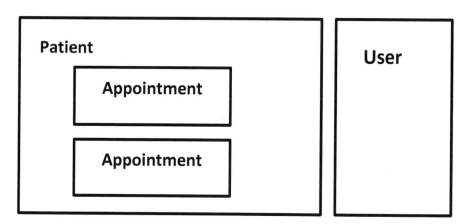

Figure 5.

A **Reception Desk Worker** would be a **User**. The diagram shown is generic, but we could, in this case, represent **Reception Desk Worker** as its own rectangle box, instead of **User**. For our purposes here, **User** is too generic.

Let's take a look at a **Swim Lane Diagram** for the process described earlier. A **Swim Lane Diagram** ties process elements to particular **Actors**. *Figure seven* on the next page shows a **Swim Lane Diagram** of the **Patient-Queue-Entry Process** described earlier. There are two actors in this process diagram: **Reception Worker** & **Patient**. The portion of the process that involves the **Patient** is located in the **Patient Lane**, and the portion of the process that involves the **Reception Worker** is in the **Reception Worker Lane**.

The "Register the Patient" process involves both **Patient** & **Reception Worker**, however, since the **Reception Worker** actually plays a more active role, the process is placed in the **Reception Worker Lane**. The actual process of registration could be complex, and potentially, one could expand on the "Register the Patient" process into its own flow. However, we need not go into that level of detail for the purpose of this book.

You might also notice that the "Patient is Asked to Come Back Later" process in the old diagram was split into two processes in the **Swim Lane Diagram**. The actual waiting belongs to the **Patient** role, whereas the request to wait belongs to the **Reception Worker** role.

Swim Lane Diagrams usually have actors on the left side, vertically (*y-axis*), as shown below:

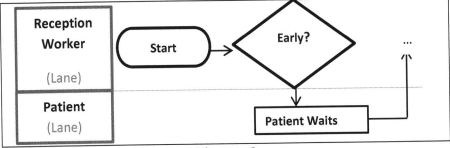

Figure 6.

To fit a **Swim Lane Diagram** nicely into a book format, we are using the top to categorize the actors—and they are categorized horizontally (*x-axis*). The concept is exactly the same--only orientation is different.

Follow the arrows to understand the below diagram. Your analysis should commence at the oval **Start** node.

Patient Queue Entry Process

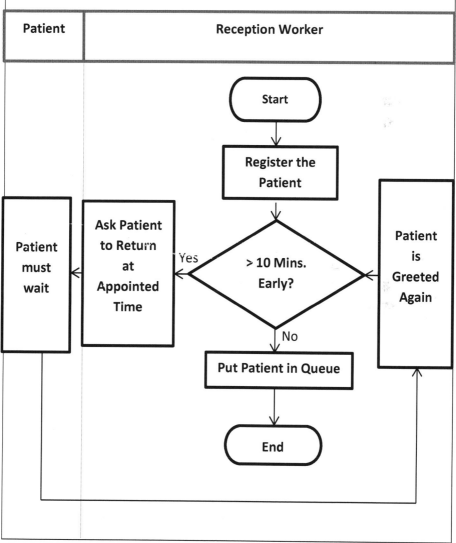

Figure 7.

Let's see if we can improve the process shown to take into account those patients that show up more than 15 minutes late. Let's ask those patients to reschedule their appointment.

See if you can come up with a new diagram that takes into account a patient showing up more than 15 minutes late. Compare it against the improved **Patient-Queue-Entry Process** in the next figure. If your flow is slightly different, it might still be valid, as often there is more than one way to get to the same end goal.

Once you finish attempting your re-design effort, turn to the next page to look at an adjusted flow diagram that takes into account a patient showing up more than 15 minutes late.

Study the new flow on the next page.

Please note that the process continues to have need for many other improvement areas.

For example, the chart implies that the patient must reschedule his appointment if he is more than 15 minutes late, but what if there is nobody in line to see the doctor at that time? It seems to make more business sense to see the patient right away.

Also, note that while "Register the Patient" process might include accepting co-pay, if later in the flow the patient is found to have shown up more than 15 minutes late, then he might be forced to re-schedule and go home after having paid his co-pay!

Our purpose, for this book, is not to create the best process, but to demonstrate the tools. Hence, we will not address all the shortcomings of the design.

However, introducing these shortcomings does give the reader a good idea about what the **Business Analyst** role entails in terms thoroughness of process analysis to ensure a good design. If the process was being designed for a real-world situation, it could be more granular, and broken down into finer detail.

Patient Queue Entry Process

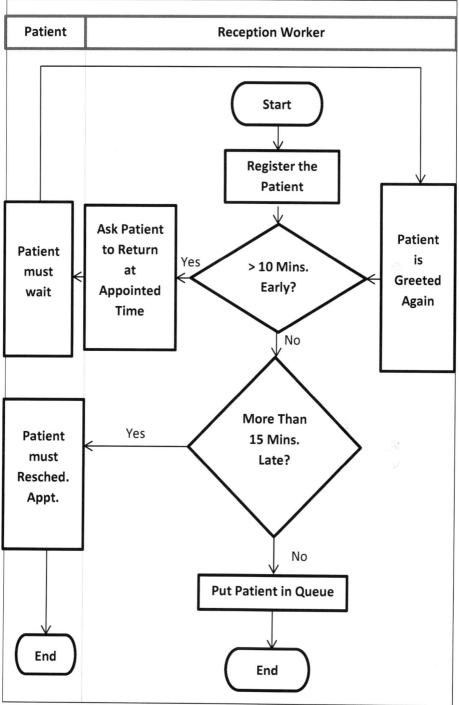

Figure 8.

Please note that in the diagram presented on prior page, the "Patient Must Reschedule" process was placed in the **Patient's Swim Lane**. Actually, the process consists of two parts: 1) **Reception Worker** must alert the patient that he must make another appointment, and 2) **Patient** must make another appointment. Since the responsibility lies primarily with the **Patient**, the process was put into the **Patient's Swim Lane**. We could have broken up the process into two pieces, if desired, and assigned **Reception Worker** the process of *alerting*, while assigning the **Patient** the process of *rescheduling*.

The **Process Flow Diagram** is one element of the **High Level Specification**. However, it must be accompanied by textual explanations. The examples we have covered in this chapter are very basic and familiar examples, and thus, I did not provide textual explanations of the flows.

Starting with the next section, we will explore **High Level Specifications** for enhancements to the **HSH** application (**Home Sweet Home**), and we will provide a complete specification, including flow descriptions.

High Level Specifications are designed based on interaction between the **BA** and the folks who relay the requirements to the **BA** (**Stakeholders**). The interaction between the **BA** and **Stakeholders** has not been shared with the reader.

The communication aspect of getting the requirements from the **Stakeholder** will be analyzed more closely in the last chapter (as well as in the **BA Role Made Easy** book, available at **BABooks.net**).

Thus far, I am only sharing knowledge on how to document information gathered from the business.

Hence, as you read each **High Level Specification**, you should come to a new understanding about the desired product—an understanding that you would have gotten through communication with the **Stakeholders**.

The book goes in order from **As-Is Flow**, **To-Be Flow**, **Use Cases**, **Screen Layout**, and finally **Test Cases**.

CHAPTER 3

High Level Specification for HSH 1.5

The Gordan Title Company is a fictional company that handles home closings throughout the United States. A **Property Closing** (also known simply as **Closing**) is a property ownership transfer event between a **Buyer** & **Seller**.

The Gordan Title Company has an application that is used to keep track of all of their home closings.

Stakeholders from the Gordan Title Company are requesting an upgrade to their **HSH 1.0** application (**Home Sweet Home 1.0**) to allow a certain category of users to be able to better scan property closing documents, and attach the documents to particular **Property Closings** (or simply **Closings**).

There are many different types of documents associated with a **Closing**. The current list of documents that are supported in **HSH 1.0** are: **Title Details**, **Property Survey**, **Seller Disclosures**, **Buyer Information**, **Seller Information**, and **Tax Assessment Details**.

Title Details is a document that describes the property location with respect to other landmarks.

Property Survey is a document that describes the property measurements and dimensions of structures (such as a home or office building) on the property.

Buyer Information is a document that specifies property buyer contact information.

Seller Information is a document that specifies property seller contact information.

Tax Assessment Details is a document that specifies the seller's tax obligations.

These are different types of documents that are attached to the **Property Closing**. Note, there is a reason why the documents are attached to the **Property Closing** *and not to the* **Property** *itself.* A property can have multiple closings (because it can shift owners several times). The various concepts associated with the document types listed (**Seller Disclosure**, **Buyer Information**, **Seller Information**, etc.) pertain to the **Closing** itself, and not to the **Property**.

There might be certain documents that can potentially reside with the property itself. For example, the **Property Survey** is a document might potentially be a static document that doesn't change very much throughout many years (typically stays the same from one owner to the next). However, there is a possibility that the **Property Survey** can also change, and for the purposes of **HSH**, all documents are stored at the **Property Closing** level, and *not at the* **Property** *level.*

The next figure shows that a property can have multiple **Closings**. That is to say, any particular property, throughout the course of its history, could potentially be served by the Gordan Title Company a multiple number of times.

Say, for example, that 123 Abe Street was closed (changed owners) five years ago by the Gordan Title Company, as well as two years ago. In other words, Gordan Title Company handled the **Closing** (ownership transfer) twice for the same property.

Each **Closing** has only one **Buyer** and one **Seller** (for the sake of simplicity). Each **Closing** has a multiple number of **Attachments**.

An **Attachment**, for our purposes, is a synonym for **Document**. The **Attachment** might be a **Property Survey**, **Seller Disclosure**, or other document (from the list of various types of documents mentioned earlier in the chapter).

Relationship between Property, Closing, Attachment, Buyer & Seller:

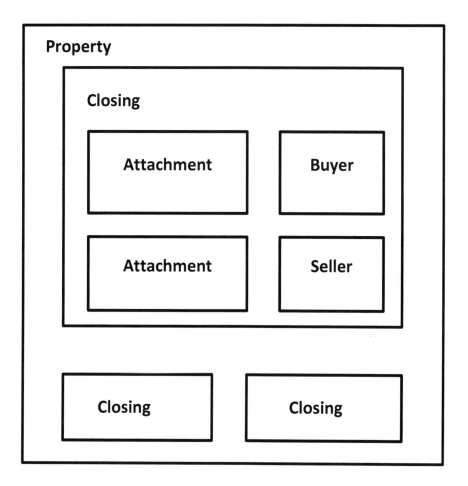

Figure 9.

Background Information needed to understand AS-IS & TO-BE Design:

A user who logs into the **HSH** system is assigned particular **Roles**. A **Role** determines certain rights and privileges that a **User** has. A **User** may have *more than one* **Role**.

If the **User** belongs to the **Doc-Manager** role, then the **User** can upload documents. All other users can view uploaded documents, but cannot upload their own documents. If a **User** belongs to **System Administrator Role**, then the user may add or change the types of documents that can be uploaded.

A particular class of users (such as **System Administrator**, **Doc-Manager**, etc.) can also be thought of as an **Actor**—specifications reference **Actors**.

AS-IS Design:

Today, **Users** cannot scan a document through **Home Sweet Home**, however, if the user belongs to the **Doc-Manager** role, the user may upload a document that has already been scanned using the scanner's scanning software. See next figure. The **Doc-Manager** a) Opens **HSH** application, b) Searches for a particular home **Closing**, c) Opens the particular **Closing** of interest, d) Switches to the **Attachments** Tab, e) Chooses the type of document to upload from the **Upload Document Type Dropdown**, f) Enters a memo description that describes the document g) Specifies the path after clicking the **Browse** button, and finally, g) Presses the **Upload** button to upload a locally scanned .pdf document. The system only allows the user to upload .pdf documents.

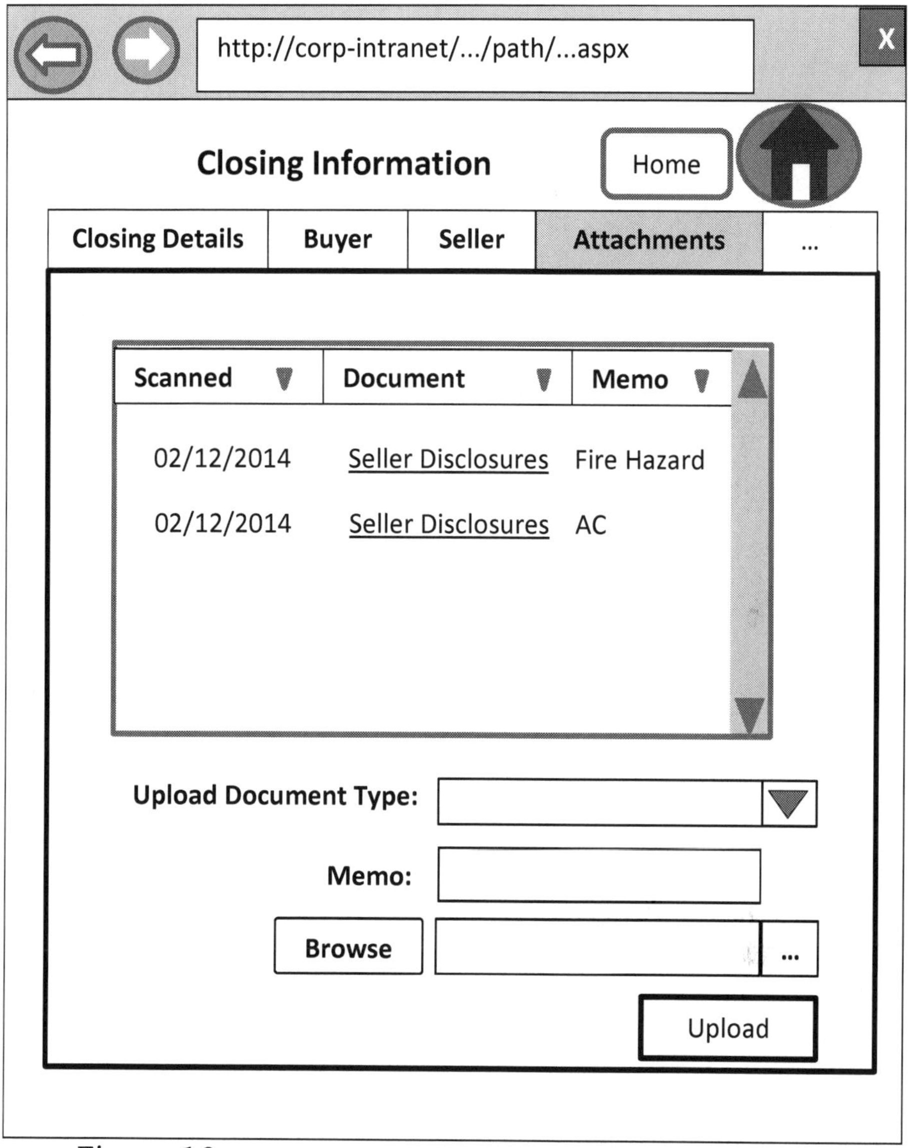

Figure 10.

The documents attached to a particular **Closing** can also be viewed through the **Attachments** Tab. The tab has a listing of documents loaded, in reverse order, by date (descending). Note that the column header indicates that the system is storing the scan date (date on which the document was actually scanned into the computer), and not the date on which the file was uploaded—the scan date will be assumed to be the date & time stamp of the file that was uploaded.

There is a column link to open up the associated .pdf. The column displays the type of document that the attachment is (**Seller Disclosure**, **Property Survey**, etc.), but every piece of data in the column is set up as a link (hence, underlined), and if clicked on, it will open up the exact document that was uploaded. The memo that the user had entered for the attachment is also displayed as a column.

The types of documents that are allowed to be uploaded (**Seller Disclosure**, **Property Survey**, etc.) are managed by **System Administrators**. Existing functionality allows any user that belongs to the **System Administrator** role to go into the system and edit document types that are supported (new document types can be added; existing document types can be decommissioned).

TO-BE Design:

We are not removing the **AS-IS** design. The **Upload Button** will remain in-tact. We are introducing a new, "Batch-scan" feature in **HSH 1.5** (**Home Sweet Home 1.5**). Instead of uploading one document at a time, the user will be allowed to scan an entire pile of attachments in one-go. The pile may contain attachments from various, different **Closings**. To identify the closing, each attachment will contain a cover sheet.

Doc-Managers (any **User** belonging to **Doc-Manager** role) can be working on many home **Closings** at the same time. In an effort to make the job of the **Doc-**

Manager very easy, the system will allow the *Doc-Manager* to print out a *Barcode Coversheet* for a particular document. A *Barcode Coversheet's* barcode will identify the *Closing* and the *Document Type* of the document to be scanned (encrypted within the barcode). Additionally, the cover sheet must also contain the following items (not encoded, in plain text):

Closing Id

Closing Date

Complete Property Address

Document Type

Barcode Sheet Example*	
The Sheet:	Description:
‖‖‖‖‖‖‖‖‖‖‖‖‖‖	← Barcode
CLS83234SD	← Closing Id
07/16/2014	← Closing Date
123 Gambit Drive	← Address & Unit (if any) (Condo.)
Houston, TX 77290	← City, State, Zip
Seller Disclosure	← Document Type.

Figure 11.   *Sheet not to scale

When scanning, the *Barcode Coversheet* will be placed first, followed by the document that is to be scanned in. Another *Barcode Coversheet* may follow

41

the set, followed by the second document that is to be scanned in. Thus, the **Doc-Manager** can scan in multiple documents at the same time for multiple different **Closings**.

The scanned documents will attach to the correct **Closings** through barcode evaluation.

Only **Doc-Managers** can scan documents into the system.

The viewing of scanned documents has not changed; it is defined in the **AS-IS** process, and the **AS-IS** process will remain intact. The only thing that we are doing in **HSH 1.5** is adding the ability to **Batch-scan**, which covers a) **Coversheet / Barcode Printing** and b) **Scanning of a Pile** of documents.

HSH (**Home Sweet Home**) is a Web-based **ASP.net** application. Web applications cannot directly print to a local printer. When printing barcode sheets, An **Adobe PDF** file will be generated and sent to the client in a new web browser window. User can choose to print the **PDF** from the browser window. When opening a **.pdf** in the browser, an **Adobe add-on** is used to open the file, which allows the user to print the file to a local printer.

Also, a web application cannot scan from a local scanner. Therefore, the **HSH** web application will invoke a local client component (non-web component) that will scan to the local computer. If scanning successfully completes, control will be passed back to the main **HSH** web application for uploading the scanned documents _from_ the client bin on the visitor's hard drive (place where scanned documents reside) _to_ the **HSH** storage repository.

When studying **AS-IS** and **TO-BE** state, you might come to note that the only thing that is changing about this application is that new **Batch-Scan** and **Barcode Print** options are being introduced to be able to facilitate scanning. Every other feature is staying intact: The manner in which the user views documents loaded in **HSH**, as well as the ability to upload .pdf documents to a particular **Closing** will remain the same in **HSH 1.5**.

High-Level Requirements Documents often include flow diagrams. We should limit the flow diagrams to 1) **AS-IS** flow of processes that will change 2) **TO-BE** flow of processes that are changing 3) **TO-BE** flow of any new processes.

Since we are not changing anything about the way individual documents would be uploaded or viewed, we will not specify a flow diagram for these features. There are no **AS-IS** processes that will change.

We will only specify the flow diagram for the new enhancements, **Barcode Print** and **Scanning of a Pile** functionalities.

The diagram for the **Barcode Print and Scan** process is much more simpler than the doctor office visit flow in the previous section. There are no decision points. There is only one swim lane, because the only role that can scan and print barcode sheets is the **Doc-Manager** role.

In a previous section, **Swim Lane Diagrams** were shown to have the various **Actors** defined at the top, along the *x-axis* (in algebra terms). This is usually not the way **Swim Lane Diagrams** are oriented—however, the information relayed is the same, whether the **Actors** are defined on the *x-axis* or *y-axis*.

Let's look at the **Barcode Print and Scan Process** in a **Swim Lane Diagram**, as it would normally be defined, with **Actors** along the *y-axis*.

Barcode Print and Scan Process

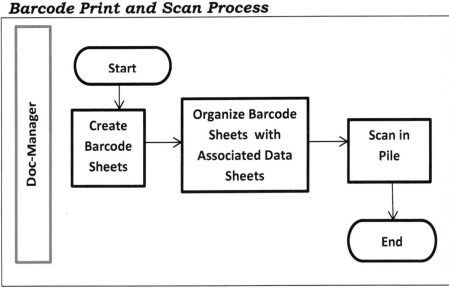

Figure 12.

Note: Any user who does not belong to the Doc-Manager Role will not have the menu option choices to be able to create barcode sheets or scan barcode sheets.

Along with the flow diagram, **High Level Specification Documentation** should provide textual explanations of the flow, as per below:

The **Doc-Manager** creates **Barcode Cover Sheets** for all **Closings** which require documentation. There is a cover sheet for each attachment. If there are two attachments of the same type for a given **Closing**, then two barcode sheets will be printed for the **Closing + Document Type** combination.

The **Doc-Manager** organizes the pile by placing a **Barcode Coversheet** at the top of the pile, followed by associated data, followed by the next **Barcode Coversheet** and associated data, etc.

The **Doc-Manager** scans in the organized pile, and the system automatically files documents to the correct **Closing** by analyzing the **Barcode Coversheet** of each document.

Barcode Coversheet has on it a barcode that tells the system which **Closing** to attach the attachment to (including **Closing Id** & **Date of Closing**). **Barcode Coversheet** does not contain information about what **Memo** the **Attachment** should have. Any special fields associated with the **Attachment**, such as **Memo**, will be kept as blank when uploading.

Only the **Doc-Manager** may perform the two functions **Print Barcode Coversheets** and **Scan Pile**.

The **High Level Specification** consists of the flow diagram, textual explanations above, as well as the detailed analysis, definitions, and illustrations covered in this section.

In essence, this entire section, apart from references to methods and techniques for documentation, can be considered as a part of the **High Level Specification Documentation**.

CHAPTER 4

Introduction to Use Cases

Use Case is a type of **BA tool** that is used to describe process flow in a greater detail than the **High Level Specification Flow** demonstrated in the previous section. A **Business Requirements Document** can have many **Use Cases**, and each **Use Case** is tied to a particular **Actor** and **Function**. The following are examples of **Use Cases** that might describe processes at a pizza restaurant:

Use Case 1: <u>Enter New Order</u>

Actor: *Order Taker*
Function: Enter New Order

Use Case 2: <u>Fulfill Order</u>

Actor: *Cook*
Function: Fulfill Order

A **Use Case** must include a) **Actor** of the case, b) the **Function** being described, and c) The **Flow** of the **Function** being described.

So far, we have not defined the flow. Let's complete the first **Use Case**—Case **Enter New Order** for **Actor Order Taker**. This is a fictional flow defined for an

Order Taker that answers the phone lines at *Papa Jake's Pizza:*

Use Case 1: <u>Enter New Order</u>

Actor: *Order Taker*
Function: Enter New Order

Flow:

1. Answer Phone.
2. Greet Customer.
3. Record Name, Number, and Delivery Method (Pick Up/Delivery) on ticket.
4. Customer chooses Delivery Method as Pick Up.
5. Record Pizza Order from Customer.
6. Give Ticket to Cook. Case Ends.

A **Use Case** may have an **Alternative Flow**. An **Alternative Flow** might be an **Exception**; an **Exception** occurs when an atypical event happens that is not in alignment with normal business flow. In the example above, an **Alternative Flow** may occur when the customer does not answer the **Order Taker's** questions.

Alternative Flow might also simply be another possible, valid business possibility. For example, the caller might choose the **Pizza Delivery** option and not the **Pizza Pick Up** option. In this particular case, the **Alternative Flow** is not truly an **Exception** because the event is not atypical—it is just another valid business possibility.

Here is an **Alternative Flow** for the scenario when the customer does not answer the request for order information:

```
┌─────────────────────────────────────────────────┐
│  Use Case 1:  Enter New Order                   │
│                                                 │
│            Actor:  Order Taker                  │
│         Function:  Enter New Order              │
│                                                 │
└─────────────────────────────────────────────────┘
```

Alternative Flow:

```
┌─────────────────────────────────────────────────┐
│  1.   Answer Phone.                             │
│  2.   Greet Customer.                           │
│  3.1  Customer does not answer the request for  │
│       order information.                        │
│  3.2  Promptly hang-up phone.  Case Ends.       │
└─────────────────────────────────────────────────┘
```

The reason why we start enumeration at 3.1 (for the third step) is because generally, there is a more concise way to represent BOTH the **Main Flow** and the **Alternative Flow**, in one list. Step 3 will continue to belong to the **Main Flow**, whereas 3.1 & 3.2 belong to the **Alternative Flow**.

Below is the concise **Case** representing both flows:

Use Case 1: <u>Enter New Order</u>

Actor: *Order Taker*
Function: Enter New Order

Flow:

1. Answer Phone.
2. Greet Customer.
3. Record Name, Number, and Delivery Method (Pick Up/Delivery) on ticket.
4. Customer chooses Delivery Method as Pick Up.
5. Record Pizza Order from Customer.
6. Give Ticket to Cook. Case Ends.

<u>Alternative Flow:</u>
a) Alternative Flow for step 3.
3.1 Customer does not answer the request for order information.
3.2 Promptly hang-up phone. Case Ends.

Note the numbering system of the alternative flow associated with step 3: 3.1 & 3.2. This is **one way** to handle enumeration for **Use Cases.** There are other, acceptable ways to handle enumeration.

On the following page, I defined **BOTH** *Alternative Flows* (Customer doesn't answer phone & Customer wants pizza delivered), concisely, within the **Use Case.**

Here is the concise **Case** representing both **Alternative Flows**; only step 4.1 & 4.2 are new—the rest is the same as before:

Use Case 1: <u>Enter New Order</u>

Actor: *Order Taker*
Function: Enter New Order

Flow:

---

1. Answer Phone.
2. Greet Customer.
3. Record Name, Number, and Delivery Method (Pick Up/Delivery) on ticket.
4. Customer chooses Delivery Method as Pick Up.
5. Record Pizza Order from Customer.
6. Give Ticket to Cook. Case Ends.

<u>Alternative Flows:</u>
a) Alternative flow for Step 3.
3.1 Customer does not answer the request for order information.
3.2 Promptly hang-up phone. Case Ends.

b) Alternative flow for Step 4.
4.1 Customer chooses the Delivery Method as Delivery.
4.2 Record Address on the ticket. Resume at step 5.

You might be able to catch some shortcomings related to flows described in this book; for example, we did not relay cost information to the customer. Once again, our focus here is more on demonstrating the tools, and you are welcome to enhance the flow as an exercise.

Alternative   Flows   can   also   contain   other *Alternative Flows*, as per *Use Case* example shown below:

Use Case 1: <u>My Fictional Use Case</u>

Actor: *Somebody*
Function: Do Something

Flow:

---

1.   Main Flow Step 1
2.   Main Flow Step 2
3.   Main Flow Step 3

<u>Alternative Flows:</u>
a)   Alternative flow for Step 2.
2.1   Step 1 of alternative for step 2
2.2   Step 2 of alternative for step 2
2.3   Step 3 of alternative for step 2

b)   Alternative flow for Step 2.2.
2.2.1   Step 1 of alternative for step 2.2
2.2.2   Step 2 of alternative for step 2.2

The enumeration technique being used in this book is as follows:

- Do not use decimal points for main flow
- In the alternative flow, the digits following the very last decimal point represent step number, and all digits prior to the last decimal point represent the step for which the flow being detailed is an alternative of. In other words, step a.b.2 is the second step of an alternative flow for step a.b.   (a.b is the ***Parent*** step).

There are times when logic can branch in such a way that there is more than one alternative path. For example, if you take a box to post office for delivery, there might be multiple choices: First Class, Ground, Air, etc.

When there is more than one branch on a step, **Alternative Paths** may take on enumeration as follows:

Use Case 1: My Fictional Use Case

Actor: *Somebody*
Function: Do Something

Flow:

1.	Main Flow Step 1
2.	Main Flow Step 2
3.	Main Flow Step 3
...	
.	
.	
S	Main Flow Step S **(First Class)**
	Alternative Flows:
a)	Alternative flow for Step S. **(Ground)**
S.1	Step 1 of alternative for step S
S.2	Step 2 of alternative for step S
S.3	Step 3 of alternative for step S
b)	Alternative flow for Step S.1 **(Air, 2 days)**
S.1.1	Step 1 of alternative for step S.1*
S.1.2	Step 2 of alternative for step S.1
c)	Alternative flow for Step S.1.1 **(Air, 1 day)**
S.1.1.1	Step 1 of alternative flow for step S.1.1**
S.1.1.2	Step 2 of alternative flow for step S.1.1

*You may think of S.1.1. as *either* step 1 of **Alternative Flow** to S.1., OR as step 1 of the **Second Alternative Flow** to S; in the case of the latter, a) represents the first alternative to Step S, and b) represents the second alternative to Step S.

You may think of S.1.1.1 as *either* step 1 of **Alternative Flow to S.1.1, OR as step 1 of the **Third Alternative Flow** to S; in the case of the latter, a) represents the first alternative to Step S, b) represents the second alternative to Step S, and c) represents the third alternative to Step S.

Once again, this is **one way** to handle enumeration for **Use Cases.** There may be other acceptable ways to handle enumeration.

Using the method employed in the book, the enumeration can get very long when dealing with scenarios that have many choices.

A Use Case may also have a **Pre-condition;** a **Pre-condition** is a condition that must be met before the case flow begins. For example, a **Pre-condition** to **Enter New Order**, for the **Actor Order Taker** could be that the **Order Taker** is manning the phone lines.

CHAPTER 5

Use Cases for HSH 1.5

Let's do the **Use Case** breakdown for printing bar-code sheets and scanning in a pile of data. As you read the **Use Cases**, you should be able to gain a greater understanding about the desired product than you had after defining the **High Level Specifications**. Many of the steps will be entirely new.

The **Use Cases** are designed based on interaction between the **BA** and the folks who relay the requirements to the **BA** (**Stakeholders**). The interaction between the **BA** and **Stakeholders** has not been shared with the reader. The communication aspect of getting the requirements from the **Stakeholder** will be analyzed more closely in the last chapter, as well as in other literature offered at **BABooks.net.**

Thus far, I am only sharing knowledge on how to document information gathered from the business.

Hence, as you read each **Use Case**, you should come to a new understanding about the desired product—an understanding that you would have gotten through communication with the **Stakeholders.**

As you read the **Alternative Flows**, you may have to move back a few pages to the step for which the alternative logic is being created.

Actor:

Doc-Manager

Function:

Generate Barcode Sheets

Pre-Condition:

User is logged into HSH

Flow:

1. User belongs to Doc-Manager Role.

2. User Selects option to Generate Barcode Sheets.

3. System presents option to Create Barcode Sheets for a particular Closing or Create Barcode Sheets for all properties that are closing on a particular date+zip code combination.

4. User chooses to Create Barcode Sheets for a particular Closing.

5. User chooses Closing Id option to provide the particular Closing (i.e. User is planning to provide Closing Id as input to identify which Closing to use).

6. User provides a particular Closing Id.

7. User chooses from document list choices: Title Details, Property Survey, Seller Disclosures, Buyer Information, Seller Information, Tax Assessment Details. User can choose to generate barcode sheets for ***one or more*** of these document types (multi-select). For example, sticking with the main flow, the user may choose to generate barcode sheets for a particular

Closing, provide the Closing Id, and choose Property Survey & Seller Disclosures as the document types. In this case, 2 barcode sheets will be generated for the Closing Id specified—Survey & Seller Disclosure.

8. User clicks the Generate Barcode Sheet button with completed input that is of a valid format.

9. Barcode sheets are generated and passed to the client in the form of PDF file that opens up in a new browser window from which user may choose to print to local printer or network printer (via Adobe add-on).

10. Go to Step 3. User stays in the web form until Close button is pressed, allowing him or her to reselect Generation options and re-press Generate Barcode Sheet button. Thus, User may generate more Barcode Sheets for additional Closings.

Alternative Flows:

1.1. User does not belong to Doc-Manager Role.

1.2. Option to Create Barcode Sheets should not be available to the user– Case ends.

4.1. User chooses to Generate Barcode Sheets for a particular date+zip code combination.

4.2. User picks date.

4.3. User picks zip.

4.4. Return to step 7 of main flow.

5.1. User chooses the Closing Address and Closing Date option to provide a particular Closing.

5.2. User provides the Closing Address & Closing Date.

5.3. Return to step 7 of core flow.

8.1. Generate Pressed, with ClosingId option selected AND also one of the following: Either missing ClosingId or ClosingId that is not formatted correctly.

8.2. Display Error Message indicating that the specified ClosingId is not of a valid format.

8.3. Resume at Step 3.

8.1.1. Generate Pressed with Address + Date option selected AND also one of the following: Either missing Address / Date field(s) OR invalid Address / Date format.

8.1.2. Display Error Message indicating that the Address / Date is not of a valid format.

8.1.3. Resume at Step 3.

9.1. The input was valid, however, based on input, no Barcode Sheets were generated.

9.2. Alert user, "There are no Closings that match your search criteria."

9.3. Resume at Step 3.

10.1. User decides to exit form by pressing Close button.

10.2. User closes from and is returned to the parent form (home screen). Case Ends.

Actor:

Doc-Manager

Function:

Scan Barcode Sheets

Pre-Condition:

User is logged into HSH

Flow:

1. User belongs to Doc-Manager Role.

2. User Selects Option to Scan Barcode Sheets.

3. Control is shifted to client application component (HSH is an ASP.net web application, and cannot support scanning functions).

4. Local HSH component detects scanners attached; at least one scanner is attached.

5. System loads a list of scanners attached.

6. User places documents on scanner of his choice.

7. There is more than one scanner attached. User picks scanner to scan from.

8. User presses button to initiate the scan.

9. Scanner scans every document into the system and saves onto local.

10. At least one document scanned in correctly.

11. Client control is terminated, and HSH upload form is invoked.

12. System displays document scan summary with links to open up .pdf version of each document scanned.

13. User opens up one or more of the .pdf links to examine whether or not the file scanned correctly.

14. By default all documents are selected as having scanned correctly, but in this step, user can deselect any documents not scanned in correctly.

15. User selects Accept button to accept the scanned documents that are selected. At least 1 document is selected.

16. Accepted documents are attached to the correct Closing(s).

17. System pops open a message indicating to the user that the scan is complete.

18. Control is re-directed to the parent screen that had invoked the Scan Barcode Sheet functionality (home screen). Case ends.

Alternative Flows:

1.1. User does not belong to Doc-Manager Role.

1.2. Option to Scan Barcode Sheets is not available – Case ends.

3.1.   Client does not have local, HSH component installed.

3.2.   Client application can't run.   Show message indicating "Cannot scan.   Client HSH Scanning component is not installed. Install now?"

3.3. User answers "Yes." Install component. Go to step 3 for retry.

3.3.1. User answers "No."

3.3.2. Option chosen to scan is aborted.

3.3.3. Control is shifted to web ASP.net HSH.

3.3.4.   User remains in web form from which option to scan was chosen (Home Screen). Case ends.

4.1. Local HSH component (client-side) does not find any scanners attached.

4.2.   System displays message indicating that no attached scanners are detected.

4.3. Client application ends.

4.4. Control is shifted to ASP.net HSH.

4.5. Option chosen to scan is aborted. User remains in web form from which option to scan was chosen (Home Screen). Case ends.

7.1 Only one scanner is attached. The scanner is pre-selected. Go to 8.

8.1. User cancels scan process from client application by pressing Cancel button.

8.2. Scanning is aborted, and client application ends.

8.3. Control is shifted to web ASP.net HSH.

8.4. User remains in web form from which option to scan was chosen (Home Screen). Case ends.

9.1. No paper is detected on scanner.

9.2. Display error indicating that no paper is detected.

9.3. Scanning is aborted but user remains in client app; continue at 6.

9.1.1. There is an unexpected scanning error of some sort.

9.1.2. Display error indicating that the nature of unexpected error (with any detail, if available).

9.1.3. Scanning is aborted but user remains in client app; continue at 6.

9.1.1.1. System does not detect valid scan-able document pile. This happens when *first page* is not a bar code sheet.

9.1.1.2. System displays error message alerting the user that the pile is not scan-able due to missing coversheet for first document.

9.1.1.3. Scanning is aborted, but user remains in client app; continue at 6.

9.1.1.1.1 Barcode coversheet encountered in scan, without data sheet.

9.1.1.1.2 Display warning, "Warning: Data sheets missing for Closing <Details>".

9.1.1.1.3 Continue Scanning rest of documents (Continue step 9). Thus, system scans what it can, and ignores what it can't scan in (ignore barcode sheets for which data-sheet is missing).

10.1. No documents are scanned successfully.

10.2. System displays error message stating that no documents were successfully scanned.

10.1.3. Go to 6 (for scan re-try).

15.1 User presses Accept button, but no documents are selected.

15.2. System alerts the user that no documents are checked off to be scanned.

15.3. User remains in document scan summary form. Goto 13.

Use Cases are not always used as the tool of choice. Many organizations like to employ the use of *Screenshots*, and not deal with *Use Cases* altogether.

A *Screenshot* is a pictorial representation of the end-product—much like the one we saw in an earlier chapter (redrawn below). Because *Screenshots* allow executives to focus on the design quickly, this is often the preferred route.

CHAPTER 6

Detailed Specs. Through UI definition

Use Cases can be used to generate *Screenshots*. Whether or not *BA's* should delve into the side of form design is a debatable issue. Although there is a school of thought that proposes that such tasks belong to software developers, business executives often prefer *Screenshots* over *Use Cases*, because they want to see the big picture quickly. In the *BA* world, we call these executives *Stakeholders*--people that feed you the requirements. *Stakeholders* are excited by *Screenshots*, and it is a valuable tool that allows them to zoom in on the design quickly. *Stakeholders* are often high level people that are short on time, and well-designed *Screenshots* are often received very well by them.

The division of labor is not always clear, and varies from one organization to another. You might end up working within an organization where the developers can design the *Screenshots* for you based on *Use-Cases* and other inputs that you provide. Sometimes, *Screenshots* are not even a part of the *Business Requirements Documentation*, especially if the project is brand new. If the project is already in production, and enhancements are being worked on, then *Screenshots* are appropriate to use.

Screenshots can be done in a variety of tools. I like to use *Microsoft Visual Studio* to create my screenshots; although it is a programming tool, mostly what I do is drag and drop controls onto the form designer—not true programming. There are many tools out there. You can even use something as simple as *Microsoft Paint,* or work with *Shapes* elements in *Microsoft Excel* or *Word* to piece together screenshots.

In my form design, I am using basic controls such as radio buttons, combo-boxes, and text boxes. The reader should be familiar with basic form design elements. If not, however, as you read the textual explanations, the purpose of the various controls on the form will become very clear.

There are 2 main functions that are new to **HSH: Barcode Generation** and **Batch Scan**.

UI Specifications consist of **Screenshots** as well as text (text that describes the screenshot function).

In the next few pages, I have provided the **Screenshot** and text for the ***Barcode Generation*** feature.

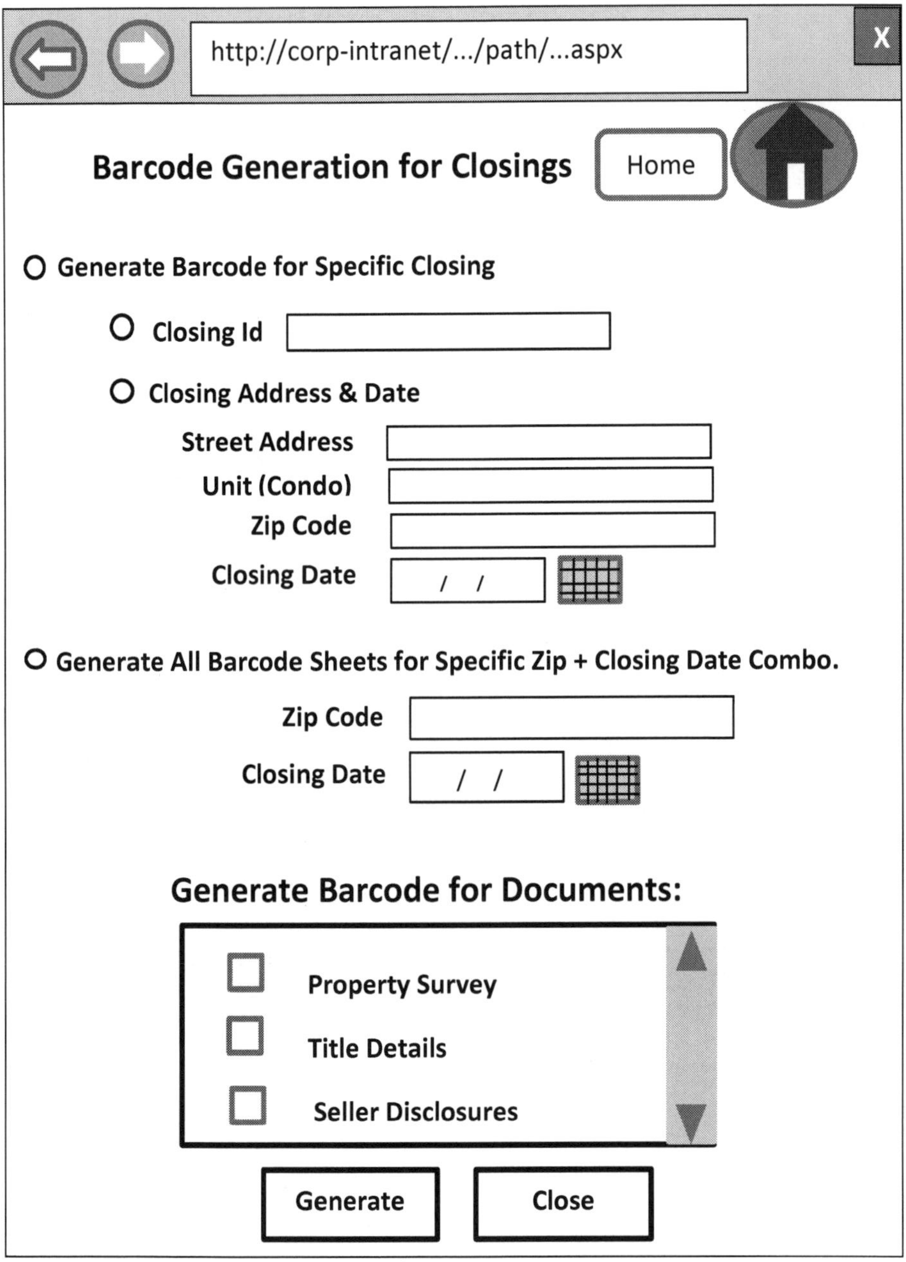

Figure 13.

If the user that is logged into the **HSH** application is a **Doc-Manager**, then he will have access to the **Barcode Generation Feature** through the **Barcode Generation Icon** on the home screen.

Once pressed, the **Barcode Generation Screen** is loaded. The user is allowed to generate **Barcode Coversheets** from this screen.

Firstly, the user must select to either generate **Barcode Coversheet(s)** for a specific closing, or to generate **Barcode Coversheet(s)** for all closings belonging to a certain **Zipcode + Closing Date** combination. The user must select the desired choice by clicking on the associated round radio button.

If the user selects the **Zipcode + Closing Date** option, then the user must specify the **Zipcode** and **Closing Date** in the respective text boxes. The **Closing Date** field also has a date control calendar button that can be clicked on to bring up a user-friendly calendar data entry input mechanism.

If, however, the user chooses to generate **Barcode Coversheets** for a specific closing, then either the user has to identify the specific closing through the **Closing Id**, or through the **Address & Closing date** input.

The user must select either the **Closing Id** or **Closing Address & Date** radio button. If the user selects **Closing Id**, then the user can freely type the **Closing Id** in the text box. If the user selects the **Address & Date** option then the user should enter the address and date field data; the Unit field is not required (used for condominium type of property). The date field has calendar button for friendly user input.

Next, the user must also specify which types of **Barcode Coversheets** to print by checking next to the appropriate **Barcode Coversheet** selection choices in the list box towards the bottom of the screen.

When the user presses the **Generate** button, the system will generate the **Barcode Coversheets**, and load the sheets into a new browser window, as a .pdf file. The user is able to print the sheets to his or her local printer from the new web browser window that pops up (through **Adobe** add-on that allows user to open web pdf documents within the browser itself).

The user can then close the **Adobe** popup web browser window, and can continue to work on the **Barcode Generation Screen**.

The user can change his or her choices and generate once again. The user remains in the form until he closes out the form through the **Close** button. Once the **Close** button is pressed, the user is returned to the **Home** page.

The user is also returned to **Home** page by pressing on Home page button.

Barcode Scan Feature:

The **Doc-Manager** must compile all data to be scanned into one pile. The first page should be a **Barcode Sheet**, followed by the related data. For example, if the first **Barcode Sheet** is about property 123 Gorham St. closing on 12/12/2013, for property *Survey Document*, then the **Doc-manager** must include the **Barcode Sheet** mentioned followed by the actual *Survey Document*, followed by the *next* **Barcode Sheet**, and the *next related document*. See example below.

Page Order Sample for Sheets to Scan In

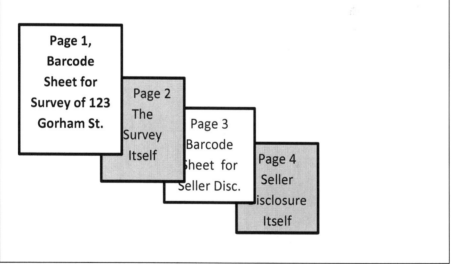

Figure 14.

Once the **Doc-manager** organizes all data into one pile, he can click the **Barcode Scan Button** from the home screen. This will launch a local, client component that sits on the user's computer (as shown in next figure).

Barcode Scan Pop Up

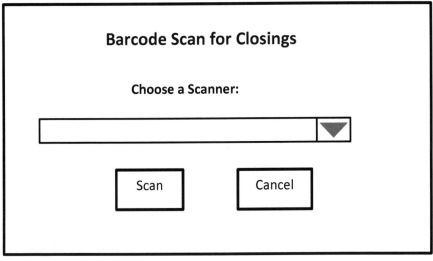

Figure 15.

The *local client component* of the application will ask the user to pick a scanner. The user must pick an attached scanner from the list, and hit the **Scan** button.

Once all documents are scanned, the **Doc-Manager** will see the list of documents detected.

Scan Validation

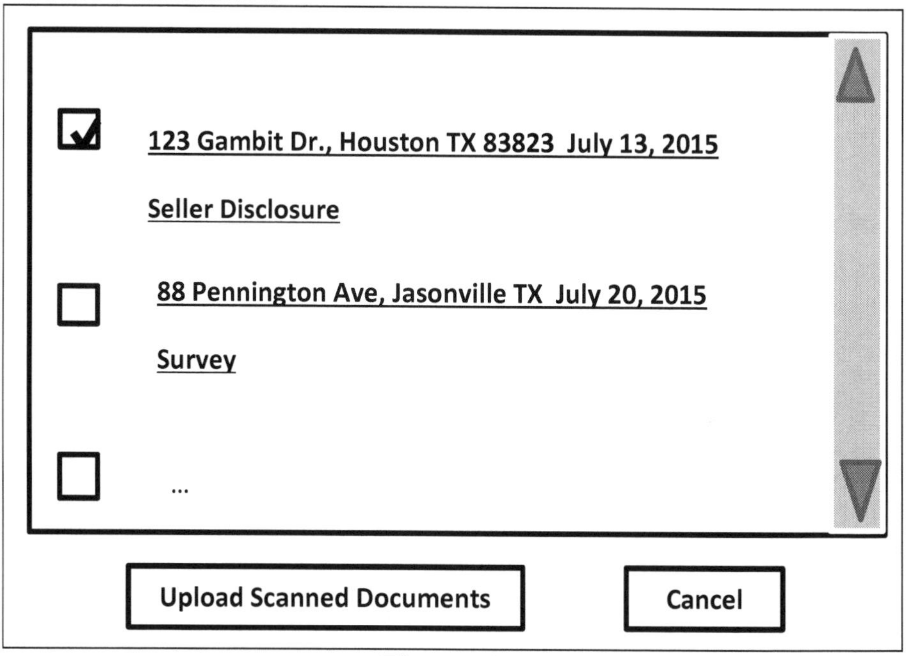

☑ **123 Gambit Dr., Houston TX 83823 July 13, 2015**

Seller Disclosure

☐ **88 Pennington Ave, Jasonville TX July 20, 2015**

Survey

☐   ...

| **Upload Scanned Documents** | **Cancel** |

Figure 16.

The user may proof the document, by clicking on the link (related .pdf will open up).

The user may place a check mark next to each document approved for upload.   By default, all documents will be approved to begin with, therefore, the user only needs to uncheck any document that is not approved.

Afterwards, the user can hit the **Upload Scanned Documents** button to attach the approved documents to the correct **Closing**.

You might notice that when we defined the **Use-Cases**, there seemed to be a lot more **Exception** handling logic provided than in the **Screenshot Design Specification**. Whether or not the **Exception** logic should be re-stated in the **Screenshot Design Specification** is a judgment call.

Stakeholders can and should sign off on the entire **Business Requirements Document**, however, **Stakeholders** might zoom in more keenly on the **Screenshot Design**, over the **Use Cases**. My experience with business **Stakeholders** is that if you give them more things to think about, your design will be held up, and your project may end up slipping schedule.

If there are certain **Exception** handling logics that are critical to the project, we should re-state those in the **Screenshot Design** text.

If your main success flow has been reviewed by the **Stakeholders**, and your main success flow covers 90% of the business scenarios, it is feasible to not re-state the **Exceptions** covered in the **Use-Cases** design; the **Stakeholders** can always read the **Use-Case** text, if they are interested. In essence, it makes good business sense to not bog down the **Stakeholders** with too much exception-handling logic, when it only covers 10% (or less) of the scenarios that will occur after product goes live (released in production).

Now, you might be thinking, *Aren't the* **Stakeholders** *the people that are feeding me the requirements and exception-handling logic in the first place?*

Answer: Yes and No. The **Stakeholders** will generally give you requirements on what they are looking for—what they are needing done. They might not go down to the level of detail related to **Exception** handling. That might be a collaborative effort between the **BA** and developers. The **Stakeholders** often prefer that the **BA** and developers do a good job of handling the **Exceptions**, and if possible, do so without involving them.

Please bear in mind that the views expressed within this book are based on practical-real-world experiences. Each organization is different, and you should flex yourself to be compatible with the methods and requirements of the organization where you work.

I will not restate all the **Exception** scenarios already covered in the **Use-cases** here. I will leave that as an optional exercise for the reader.

CHAPTER 7

Test Cases

A **Test Case Document** is used by software testers to test an application.

Test cases are basically different scenarios / test points based on the **Regular Work-flow** as well as **Exceptions**. **Regular Work-flow** refers to normal, successful program operation (including **Main** & **Alternative** flows—tying back to **Use Cases**).

Here is an example of a Regular Work Flow: The user puts a pile of properly compiled sheets for scanning, and the system scans those in and presents the user with an upload form.

The behavior described above is exactly the main purpose of the program—a successful scan of a pile of documents.

Exceptions are situations that occur *outside the normal, success scenario. For example, if the first page scanned does not have a barcode on it, then the system might reject the pile with an error message.* That would be an **Exception** scenario.

To create **Test Cases**, one has to reference the requirements, taking into account **both, Use Cases** as well as the **Screenshot** design. Occasionally, the screen flow might provide a slightly different flow from the one envisioned by the *Use Cases*, however, functionally, the screen flow will not be lacking in any way. The actual screen design must *include all functionality* that the *Use Cases* are striving to specify.

Use Cases might contain more *Exception* detail than the *Screenshot Specifications*, as is the case in our example for the *Barcode Scan* option.

The creation of test cases is not rocket science. *Test Cases* are basically a reflection of the various scenarios that a user can perform to validate that the system is behaving according to expectations. The creation of test cases relies on the ability to understand the system behavior, as well as document the various possibilities in table-format.

I have included some test scenarios for the *Barcode Generation* function in this document. As you read the test cases, you will see that the scenarios are directly related the various system behaviors already defined in the *Use-Cases* and *Screenshot Specifications* text.

I will leave it to the reader to come up with the rest of the scenarios for the project (Hint: Go back to the *Use-Cases & Screenshots*—they will practically give you your answer!)

In the process of writing test cases, it is possible for the *BA* to think of new scenarios *that are not defined in either* the *Use-Cases Specification* or the *Screenshot Specifications*. Those scenarios should be added into the test case document.

Feature	Case	Steps	Expectation
Barcode Printing	Launch by Doc-Manager	Precondition: User is logged in; user is Doc-Manager. 1. Press on the Barcode Printing Icon from home screen	The Barcode Print Screen should launch.
Barcode Printing	Launch by user that is not Doc-Manager	Precondition: User is logged in; user is not a Doc-Manager. 1. Option to press the Barcode Printing Icon from the home screen is not available.	The Barcode Print Screen cannot be launched.
Barcode Printing	Print a Barcode for a particular Closing Id	Precondition: User is logged in as Doc-Manager, and has launched Barcode Print Screen via Icon. 1. Select "Generate Barcode Sheet for Specific Closing" option. 2. Select Closing Id option 3. Specify Closing Id 4. Specify one or more Barcode Sheet types to print in the list box. 5. Hit the Generate button and ensure the .pdf contains all cover sheets expected.	System should generate Barcode Cover Sheets for only the Closing Id specified, and should print all the Barcode Cover Sheets for those document types identified.
...	...	...	...

CHAPTER 8

Building Confidence

The **Business Analyst** role is not necessarily a complex profession such as a nuclear scientist or physicist. If you have a mind that is able to think about things logically, the role of **BA** may be suitable for you.

But it does take skills, and those skills are developed over time. As you might have noticed in this book, the ideas that had been brainstormed weren't altogether difficult to understand and follow. Sometimes, it is difficult to think of good ideas, however, with time, patience, and experience, you can think of good solutions to business challenges.

The **BA** role is not limited to the experienced. It is a growing field, and there is room for **BA's** of all levels—from entry level to senior.

Requirements are based on interaction between the **BA** and the folks who relay the requirements to the **BA** (**Stakeholders**).

Here are some tips that I learned over time...

Do not be alarmed if you get into a room of **Stakeholders**, and whatever they say goes above your head—you can't understand what they are saying. Remember, they have been doing their job for many,

many years. You are a new-comer to their practices and processes. They might be using words that you are not familiar with, or they might be talking faster than you can think!

Strive to work with each **Stakeholder** in 1-1 (one to one) meetings. In other words, you should have a separate meeting with each **Stakeholder**. This helps the **BA** tremendously.

When you get into a room of **Stakeholders**, the **Stakeholders** might talk above your head, and start to drive the meeting, while you are miles behind striving to understand what someone just said five minutes ago.

When you talk with a **Stakeholder** independently, you can slow her down, ask questions, and understand the processes better. You can even ask the **Stakeholder** to define words that she assumed you had already known.

Drawing pictures and flows on paper during discussion is often helpful, as sometimes pictures are easier to follow than words.

Secondly, remember that **Stakeholders** are looking for solutions to problems and challenges. Although they can provide to you the exact solution or process improvement that they are looking for, there's no reason why you can't propose your own idea for a solution.

In the second section, we were able to find numerous flaws in the design chosen for processing patients into a queue at a doctor's office. By careful thinking, one can propose an optimal solution, and sometimes even a better solution than what the **Stakeholder** had proposed!

As long as you are able to remain humble about sharing your ideas, the **Stakeholder** will be happy to consider your solution. Propose your solution as a question: *How about if we do it this way, instead....*

I hope this book was beneficial to you. I would definitely like to hear from my readers. If you've gone this far in the text, I would appreciate it if you can go to **Amazon.com** and write a book review of the text.

You may also send feedback independently by contacting the author at BA Books (http://BABooks.net); the author's contact email will be at the top of the web page. Please put "BA Feedback" in the subject line. I will personally answer your questions, and I can use your comments to improve the book.

Made in the USA
Lexington, KY
25 June 2017

Business Analyst
Quick Start Guide

http://babooks.net